Thunderstorms

JIM AND RONDA REDMOND

Raintree

Nature on the Rampage

www.raintreepublishers.co.uk

Visit our website to find out more information about **Raintree** books.

To order:
☎ Phone 44 (0) 1865 888112
🖹 Send a fax to 44 (0) 1865 314091
🖥 Visit the Raintree Bookshop at www.raintreepublishers.co.uk to browse our catalogue and order online.

First published in Great Britain by Raintree Publishers, Halley Court, Jordan Hill, Oxford, OX2 8EJ, part of Harcourt Education.
Raintree is a registered trademark of Harcourt Education Ltd.

Consultants: Dr. Len Keshishian, State University of New York; Maria Kent Rowell, Sebastopol, California; David Larwa, National Science Education Consultant, Michigan

Cover Design: Jo Sapwell and Michelle Lisseter
Production: Jonathan Smith

Originated by Dot Gradations
Printed and bound in China and Hong Kong by South China

ISBN 1 844 21215 7
07 06 05 04 03
10 9 8 7 6 5 4 3 2 1

British Library Cataloguing in Publication Data
Redmond, Jim
Thunderstorms. – (Nature on the Rampage)
1.Thunderstorms – Juvenile Literature
551.5'54
A catalogue for this book is available from the British Library

Acknowledgements
The publishers would like to thank the following for permission to reproduce photographs:
Bettmann/Corbis, p. 22. Digital Stock, pp. **1, 8, 13, 14, 18, 20, 29**.Darrel Plowes, p. **4**. Photo Network, p. **24**. South Dakota Tourism/Charles Williams, p. **7**; Chad Coppess, p. **26**. Unicorn Stock Photos/Art Gurmankin, p. **16**

Cover photograph by Getty Images

Contents

Most thunderstorms are less than 30 kilometres (20 miles) wide.

When the sky darkens

Every year, there are more than 16 million thunderstorms around the world. These storms are violent rainstorms with thunder and lightning. At any given time, about 2000 thunderstorms are happening somewhere on the Earth's surface. Around 100 lightning bolts strike the ground every second.

Thunderstorms happen most often in the spring and summer. They can be big or small. Some are just a few kilometres wide, while others can be hundreds of kilometres across. Most are no wider than 3 kilometres (2 miles). The average thunderstorm is 24 kilometres (15 miles) wide and lasts for about 30 minutes. Ten per cent of thunderstorms lead to high winds, flash floods or tornadoes, which cause more damage than the lightning and rain alone.

What are thunderstorms like?

Thunderstorms are powerful. In just 20 minutes, a thunderstorm can drop 470 million litres of water. It can also release more electrical energy through lightning than people in a large city use during a whole week.

Clouds are low in the sky during a thunderstorm. They are often dark, almost black. Clouds get dark because they are made of millions of tiny water drops, which stop sunlight from passing through. The more rain a cloud is holding, the darker it is.

Even though rain forms in the clouds, it does not always strike the ground during a thunderstorm. Sometimes the air below the cloud is so dry that the water evaporates before it hits the ground. To evaporate is to change to vapour. Water in gas form is called water vapour.

Strong winds can blow during a thunderstorm because of the movement of warm and cool air. Warm air flows up from the ground to the cloud in an **up-draught**. Cold air is blown from the cloud to the ground in a **down-draught**.

▲ Clouds grow dark during a thunderstorm because they hold so much rain.

Sometimes a thunderstorm's rising warm air begins to spin. It is then called a cyclone. This can turn into a tornado. A tornado is a twisting, funnel-shaped column of air with winds of up to 480 kilometres (300 miles) per hour. The end of the funnel touches the ground and can cause massive destruction.

▲ A tornado has formed from spinning winds inside this powerful thunderstorm.

What does a thunderstorm do?

Thunderstorms can bring hail. **Hailstones** form when tiny ice crystals in a cloud become coated with water. An up-draught carries these crystals to high levels in the cloud, where the water freezes. The hailstones repeat this process until they become heavy and fall from the cloud towards the Earth.

There is always lightning during a thunderstorm. Lightning kills more people than tornadoes do. Lightning can strike trees, houses and people. It also causes forest fires.

Thunderstorms can cost people millions of pounds each year. Their strong winds can blow down tree branches and damage buildings. Hailstones from powerful thunderstorms can grow as large as tennis balls. Large hailstones knock down crops, crack roofs and kill animals or people.

Some thunderstorms cause flash floods. These sudden floods happen when large amounts of rain fall in a short period of time. Usually, the rain water drains into a river, which then overflows its banks. The water can then run over fields or even into people's houses.

Thunderstorms over the ocean can cause hurricanes or tropical storms. Hurricanes can be hundreds of kilometres wide, with wind speeds of up to 320 kilometres (200 miles) per hour.

This thunderstorm is happening in the evening, after the ground has been warmed by the sun all day.

Causes of thunderstorms

An atmosphere surrounds the Earth. The Earth's atmosphere is made up of layers of gas, including oxygen. People need the oxygen in the atmosphere to breathe. Powerful winds often form in the atmosphere as gases move about. Air in the atmosphere is always moving. This movement causes different kinds of weather.

Almost all storms happen when large masses of air meet. An **air mass** is a body of air with the same temperature and amount of water vapour throughout. The edges where these air masses meet are called **fronts**. Thunderstorms form when a warm air mass meets a cold air mass. Instead of mixing, they push against each other.

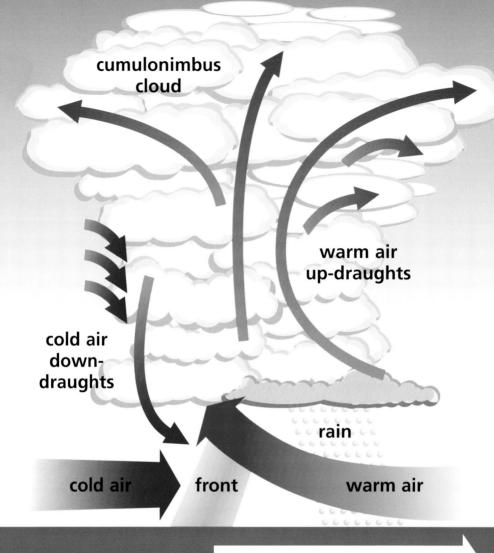

cumulonimbus cloud

warm air up-draughts

cold air down-draughts

rain

cold air

front

warm air

land

direction of storm travel

This diagram shows how thunderstorms form.

 Do you know how to tell how far away a thunderstorm is? After a lightning flash, count the seconds until you hear the sound of thunder. Divide this number by three. This number roughly shows how far away the thunderstorm is. This is because you see the lightning almost immediately. But the sound of thunder takes about three seconds to travel 1 kilometre.

How a thunderstorm forms

When air moves, clouds can form. Warm air is usually wet. Cool air is usually dry and heavier than warm air. When warm air and cool air meet, the warm air rises until it cools. When warm air cools, the moisture forms water droplets that join together to make cumulus clouds. These clouds look like big balls of cotton wool. They rise from 600 to 3000 metres high.

Thunderstorms happen most often in the afternoon or evening. This is because the air near the ground has been warmed all day by the sun. This warm air rises and meets cool air higher in the atmosphere.

▲ This supercell storm has formed from a huge cumulonimbus cloud.

Supercells

A **supercell** is the largest and most dangerous kind of thunderstorm. Supercells can last for hours and travel hundreds of kilometres.

Supercells are made up of cumulonimbus clouds. These clouds grow from cumulus clouds. As warm, moist air keeps rising, cumulus clouds grow upwards and spread out. They form cumulonimbus clouds. These clouds can reach from 1500 to over 15,000 metres high. A supercell is made of several **thunderheads,** or cells, that come together. A cell is a cylinder of rising and falling air.

A supercell has a deep, turning **up-draught** called a **mesocyclone**. A mesocyclone is a column of swirling air that rises at speeds of up to 270 kilometres (170 miles) per hour. This rising air stops rain from falling and makes the supercell get larger and larger. Tornadoes can form from the rising and swirling air in a supercell.

Supercells also have strong **down-draughts** of cold wind that are blown to the ground when the warm air rises. These winds can reach 160 kilometres (100 miles) per hour. Sometimes down-draughts can do as much harm as a tornado.

Falling rain or hail eventually creates a cold down-draught along the ground. This cool wind stops the rising warm air. Without warm air to feed the cell, the clouds break up and the thunderstorm gradually ends.

These lightning bolts were created by energy inside the thunderheads.

Thunder and lightning

Thunderstorms release a great deal of energy. The violent moving air inside the storms creates static electricity in the clouds. Raindrops and ice crystals smash into each other and spread the energy throughout the clouds. Up to 1 million volts of electricity can build up in each square metre of a thunderhead. A volt is a measure of the force of an electrical current or flow. The clouds release this energy as lightning. Each second, about 100 lightning bolts strike somewhere on the Earth.

No two lightning bolts are alike. A bolt of lightning can be up to 8 kilometres (5 miles) long but is usually only 1 to 5 centimetres wide.

▲ **This forked lightning is jumping from cloud to cloud.**

How lightning moves

Lightning may have up to 1000 million volts of energy, which makes it one of the most powerful forces on the Earth.

Lightning can jump from cloud to cloud, from cloud to ground or from ground to cloud. Some lightning occurs within one cloud or in the air.

Lightning electrifies the air it passes through. It always finds the easiest path from the cloud to the ground. If it strikes the ground, lightning usually hits the tallest object in the area.

Types of lightning

There are different types of lightning. Four examples of lightning are forked, ribbon, sheet and ball lightning. Forked lightning has one main arm that shoots down. When this arm nears the ground, it branches out into two or more zigzagged forks. Sometimes forked lightning looks like a flowing string and is called ribbon lightning.

Sheet lightning happens when lightning stays inside a cloud. The sky glows when this happens. When people see it in a storm that is far away, it is called heat lightning. Then it looks like a cloud flashing in the sky.

Ball lightning is the rarest and strangest kind of lightning. It is about 30 centimetres wide. It looks like a bright red or yellow ball of light floating in the air before it bursts.

Did you know that the chances of being hit by lightning are one in 600,000? But lightning struck a man called Roy Sullivan seven times. Once he lost his big toenail. Another time, his eyebrows were burnt off. His hair caught fire twice. Amazingly, he lived through the lightning strikes.

This lightning bolt has heated the air around it, causing the sound of thunder.

Thunder

Thunder is the sound made by air that is heated by a lightning flash. In one-fifth of a second, lightning heats the air around it up to 30,000°C. This is five times hotter than the surface of the Sun.

Air is made up of tiny pieces called molecules. The molecules heat up so quickly that they crash into each other and make sound waves. These sound waves are thunder. People can hear thunder from up to 15 kilometres (10 miles) away in the right conditions.

People hear thunder after they see the lightning that causes it. This is because sound travels much slower than light. Sound travels through air at 0.32 kilometres (0.2 miles) per second, while light travels at nearly 300,000 kilometres (186,000 miles) per second. For every kilometre (0.6 miles) away lightning is, it takes three seconds to hear the thunder.

Thunder sounds different depending on how far away it is. When it is close, it sounds like a sharp clap. When it is far away, thunder makes a rumbling noise, because the sound waves travel through the different layers of the atmosphere at different speeds.

People once believed the god Thor made thunder and lightning.

Studying thunderstorms

Before people understood how storms worked, they made up myths, or stories, about them. Many myths tried to explain how thunder and lightning happened.

In ancient Greece, people believed that one-eyed giants made lightning for the god Zeus. People thought that Zeus threw lightning bolts at the Earth when he was angry.

In Scandinavia, people believed thunder came from the god Thor. Lightning came when he threw his magic hammer. Thunder boomed as he rode his chariot over the clouds.

Now scientists can use tools and instruments to study the weather and explain why thunderstorms happen. It is even possible to predict when a thunderstorm will strike an area of land.

▲ This meteorologist is using information from radar to make a weather forecast.

Different ways to study weather

Meteorology is the study of weather. Scientists who study the weather are called **meteorologists**. Meteorologists try to forecast, or predict, what the weather will be like at a certain time. They use different instruments to gather information and make their forecast as accurate as possible.

Doppler radar machines send out energy waves called radio waves to find out how far away a storm is. The radio waves bounce off **precipitation** and travel back to a radar unit. Precipitation is any form of water that falls from the sky, including rain, snow, sleet and hail. The time it takes for the radio waves to come back tells the scientist how far away the storm is. Doppler radar can also measure wind speed and the amount of rainfall.

Weather **satellites** are spacecraft that carry special scientific instruments. They circle the Earth, take pictures of clouds and send them back to the Earth. Meteorologists study these pictures to see where storms are starting to form.

Storm chasers also study the weather. These people get as close to a storm as possible. That way, they can see close up what happens in a storm. They take photographs and films of storms. They record weather data, including rainfall and wind speed. Some storm chasers fly aeroplanes through the middle of thunderstorms and hurricanes.

▲ The sky often grows dark before a thunderstorm.

Warnings

People can avoid being caught outside during a thunderstorm by knowing the warning signs. The sky often darkens before a thunderstorm. Lightning flashes and thunder may rumble. It can also become windy. If these things happen, people should find shelter straight away.

The safest place during a thunderstorm is inside a strong building or car. These places offer protection from rain, hail, wind and lightning. Stay away from windows, which might be shattered by flying debris. Turn off electrical things like televisions and avoid using the telephone. These can be dangerous during a storm because they provide a route for lightning to travel into a building. Stay away from running water in the house as lightning can travel through water.

It is very dangerous to be outside during a thunderstorm. People struck by lightning or large hailstones can die. Stay away from tall things, such as trees and telephone poles, because they can be hit by lightning and fall over. It is dangerous to be in a high place or an open field. Lightning bolts strike metal and water too, so keep away from metal objects, as well as rivers and lakes.

Lightning can strike the same place twice, and often does. During one storm, the Empire State Building in New York was hit fifteen times in the same number of minutes. Most tall buildings today have lightning conductors that allow electricity to pass harmlessly to the ground without damaging the building.

The future

Some meteorologists think the number of storms may be increasing because of global warming. Global warming describes how temperatures on Earth are rising because of the greenhouse effect. Scientists think that the amount of carbon dioxide and moisture in the atmosphere is increasing. Carbon dioxide is a gas that is pumped into the air by cars, factories and burning fossil fuels. The carbon dioxide and water vapour form a layer around the Earth and stop some of the Sun's warmth from leaving our atmosphere every year. This slowly raises the temperature on the Earth.

Temperatures have already risen over the Earth's oceans. At the same time, more tropical storms and hurricanes have been happening. Scientists think global warming might be causing more of these storms to form. They hope to keep studying this link between global warming and storms to understand what weather will be like in the future.

▲ **A deadly tornado blew down
these buildings.**

Thunderstorms that develop into tornadoes and hurricanes cause more damage to the Earth and people than any other thing in nature. Tornadoes and hurricanes are deadly. Meteorologists cannot stop thunderstorms from happening. But it is important for them to forecast the weather. That way, they can give people earlier warnings. Better warnings help save people's lives.

Glossary

air mass body of air with the same temperature and amount of water vapour throughout

down-draught downwards-blowing wind

front edge of a large air mass where it meets another air mass

hailstone chunk of ice that falls from a storm cloud

mesocyclone (me-soh-SYE-clohn) very strong, twisting up-draught of warm air

meteorologist scientist who studies weather

precipitation any form of water that falls from the sky, including hail, snow and rain

satellite spacecraft with scientific instruments that orbits the Earth

supercell very large thunderstorm formed when smaller thunderstorm cells develop into a swirling storm with a powerful up-draught and down-draught

thunderhead rounded mass of cumulus cloud often appearing before a thunderstorm

up-draught upwards-blowing wind

Addresses and Internet sites

Met Office
London Road
Bracknell
Berkshire, RG12 25Z

Met Office Website
www.metoffice.gov.uk/education/curriculum/
  leaflets/thunderstorms

BBC Weather Centre
www.bbc.co.uk/weather/weatherwise/factfiles/
  extremes/storms

Clouds R Us.com
www.rcn27.dial.pipex.com/cloudsrus/thunder

Commonwealth Bureau of Meteorology
www.bom.gov.au/lam/climate/levelthree/
  c20thc/storm

Index